Original title:
Laughter Under the Canopy

Copyright © 2025 Creative Arts Management OÜ
All rights reserved.

Author: Gideon Shaw
ISBN HARDBACK: 978-1-80567-216-6
ISBN PAPERBACK: 978-1-80567-515-0

Playful Breezes and Heartfelt Grins

In the shade where shadows dance,
Giggles float like leaves in chance.
Squirrels chatter, playing tricks,
While sunlight plays with nature's mix.

Bubbles rise from joy, not fear,
As whispered jokes are passed from ear.
The earth beneath us is alive,
In this glee, we laugh and thrive.

Each breeze tickles with a tease,
And joy is wafted with such ease.
We bounce like sprites, with hearts aglow,
In this bright world, time's set to flow.

Chimes of Laughter Through the Wood

Whispers of joy echo all around,
As playtime spirits dance on the ground.
A chorus of chuckles, sweet and clear,
Sounds of delight that all can hear.

Tree branches sway with a knowing grin,
As playful banter whirls within.
Mismatched socks on a dandelion ground,
Spin a tale of hilarity profound.

A raccoon peeks with a curious glare,
While hectic squirrels frolic without care.
Leaves rustle in giggles, what a treat,
A whimsical world beneath our feet.

Sunlit Snickers by the Stream

By the water's edge, we find our glee,
With splashes bright and a playful spree.
Ducklings waddle, their tails a-flap,
Leading to laughter, a joyful map.

Frogs jump high, their croaks fit for jest,
In this moment, we are truly blessed.
Sunbeams shine on every grin,
As ripples of joy make our heads spin.

Bubbles ascend to the azure sky,
With each lost giggle, the seagulls sigh.
Nature's comedy plays on repeat,
As we savor this joy, bittersweet.

Revelry Amidst the Bark and Foliage

Through tangled vines, our laughter rings,
Where every step, the forest sings.
A jester's cap on a tree trunk bold,
Hides secrets of laughter yet untold.

Flowers giggle in colors bright,
As butterflies dance in sheer delight.
The canopy sways, a boisterous cheer,
Welcoming whimsies that draw us near.

A rabbit bounds with a cheeky leap,
While shadows play in the woods so deep.
In this wild kingdom, we claim our throne,
In moments where joy is fully grown.

Humming Hearts in Hidden Places

In the shade where secrets hide,
Butterflies twirl on a playful ride.
Squirrels chatter, a comic spree,
Nature's jesters, wild and free.

Bubbles of giggles from leafy sprites,
Echoing softly through sunny bites.
Rabbits hop with a silly flair,
Tickling the grass, without a care.

The breeze sings tunes of laughter bright,
As the sun dances, a radiant light.
Whimsical shadows prance and sway,
In this realm where joys hold sway.

Jolly Whispers in the Woodland

Beneath the boughs, a raucous scene,
Foxes frolic, their eyes agleam.
Chirping birds with hints of jest,
Celebrate life, among the rest.

The mushrooms giggle, yellow and round,
While fireflies blink, illuminating the ground.
Trees share secrets, a rustling sound,
As woodland creatures gather 'round.

A raccoon wearing a makeshift hat,
Wobbles and tumbles, then rolls on the mat.
Joy spills over like morning dew,
In this woodland of cheer, for me and for you.

The Happy Chorus by the Old Oak

Old Oak stands with a knowing grin,
As chipmunks dance and spin like the wind.
A chorus of chuckles fills the air,
Where nature's mischief brings perfect flair.

Acorns drop like playful stunts,
While bouncy fawns explore their haunts.
The old tree sways, applause ensues,
For every creature in vibrant hues.

Beneath its limbs, they share a jest,
Finding treasures from nature's chest.
With every squeak and playful shout,
The echoes of joy are never in doubt.

Mirrored Smiles of Nature's Play

In a pond where reflections gleam,
Frogs croak out a jubilant theme.
Their voices ripple, a cheerful show,
As reeds sway gently, joining the flow.

Ladybugs giggle on soft petals,
Dances of joy as the sunlight settles.
The wind whispers tricks as it twirls,
Making leaves spin in joyful swirls.

Each sunrise brings a fresh delight,
Nature's canvas, painted bright.
From every nook, a smile can peek,
In this tapestry, funny and unique.

Freedom and Fun in the Forest

In the woods where the wild things play,
Squirrels dance in a cheeky ballet.
Frogs croak jokes on lily pads near,
While the sun tickles leaves, spreading cheer.

Rabbits race with a hop and a skip,
Chasing shadows, they giggle and trip.
The breeze sings tunes, a playful tune,
While bees buzz laughter, just like a cartoon.

Under the branches, all nature's bright,
Every rustle brings pure delight.
A woodpecker's tap is the beat of the day,
In this merry realm, we all come out to play.

Graciously Goofy in the Grove

Amidst the trees, a whimsical sight,
A raccoon in glasses reads by candlelight.
The owls crack jokes, wise and absurd,
While turtles tumble, and laughter is stirred.

Dancing mushrooms, with caps all aglow,
Invite the ants to join in the show.
A wiggly worm does the cha-cha with glee,
As the sun whispers secrets to each leafy tree.

A pig in a tutu rolls down the hill,
With giggles and squeals, they bring such a thrill.
In this goofy grove, where joy is the tone,
Every creature finds laughter, never alone.

The Blissful Boughs of Belonging

Beneath the trees, where friendships bloom,
A parrot spins tales, dispelling all gloom.
The chipmunks gather, their stories unfold,
Of mischief and fun that never grows old.

A bear in a hat makes a clumsy debut,
Trips over roots, but smiles shine right through.
The whispers of leaves echo laughter near,
In this cozy nook, joy's always near.

Fireflies twinkle like stars in the night,
As crickets compose a serenade bright.
Under the boughs, we dance and we sing,
In this circle of friends, happiness takes wing.

Joy's Revel from the Canopy

High in the treetops, a party begins,
Where the breezes giggle and joy never thins.
Monkeys swing wildly, flipping with flair,
As harmony bubbles up into the air.

Pine cones collide, like clattering cheer,
The squirrels add rhythm from branches up here.
With every twist, every turn we engage,
The heart of the forest bursts open with stage.

The shadows giggle, the sunlight grins wide,
Nature's essence, a jubilant ride.
Under these leaves, we frolic and spin,
Together in joy, where all lives begin.

The Playful Pulses of the Woods

Beneath the leafy, swaying crowns,
The squirrels dance in funny gowns.
With acorns tossed into the air,
Their playful antics draw a stare.

A rabbit hops, then takes a bow,
While birds serenade the furry crowd.
Each rustle brings a chuckling breeze,
As nature holds her light-hearted tease.

The brook chuckles, gurgling free,
Tickling rocks with glee and glee.
Every splash a joke is spun,
A joyous game has now begun.

Listen closely, hear the cheer,
Echoing well from far and near.
The woods alive with giggling sounds,
In this realm where joy abounds.

Harmonies of Happiness Among the Trees

In twilight's glow, the shadows play,
As giggles leap from trees at play.
An owl blinks, with a wink so sly,
While whispers sing from birds that fly.

A raccoon's prance, a playful jest,
While crickets chirp, they do their best.
Each note a laugh upon the air,
In this green world, without a care.

Wind tickles leaves, they rustle and sway,
Branches sway like children at play.
Beneath the stars, hearts take flight,
In nature's song, all feels just right.

So gather 'round, both young and old,
For tales of joy and laughter bold.
Under these skies, we're free and bright,
In harmony, our spirits take flight.

Revelry in the Rays of Radiance

Sunbeams stretch like playful arms,
Inviting all to share their charms.
A butterfly twirls in bright delight,
While shadows jiggle in the light.

The daisies nod, they're part of the fun,
As giggles tickle each speck of sun.
The brook bounces, claps its hands,
In frothy curls, where laughter fans.

Gentle breezes join the dance,
Whispering tales of nature's chance.
The air is filled with sweet refrain,
Echoing life's joyful train.

As dusk approaches, the stars align,
Each glimmer sharing tales divine.
In this fair realm, the world feels grand,
Where mirth and magic always stand.

Sunshine and Snickers

In the meadow where shadows play,
A squirrel slips, what a funny way!
The flowers giggle in the sun's embrace,
As butterflies flutter with a silly grace.

Beneath the branches, whispers fly,
A rabbit trips, oh my, oh my!
The creek chuckles with a bubbling song,
As nature dances, where we belong.

Echoes of Cheer in the Forest

Amidst tall trees where branches swing,
A whoop from a bird makes the forest sing.
A raccoon makes faces, peeking about,
While friendly woodpeckers join in with a shout.

The leaves above shimmy, sway, and twirl,
As woodland critters give laughter a whirl.
A deer prances by, with a wag of its tail,
In this cheerful glade, joy will prevail.

The Dance of Delighted Shadows

Silhouettes leap in the golden light,
Bumbling shapes swirling to a silly height.
A gopher pops up with a cheeky grin,
While sunlight tickles the roots from within.

The shadows stretch long as a breeze begins,
And laughter erupts where the fun never thins.
A fox in a hat tells a jester's tale,
Creating ripples in this joyous trail.

Joyful Revelry Among the Roots

Between the roots where young sprouts hide,
A trio of frogs goes for a wild ride.
They leap and they croak, in a comic spree,
While the wise old owl shakes his head in glee.

The groundhog rolls, what a sight to see,
Chasing after butterflies, carefree as can be.
With each little chuckle and every loud cheer,
Nature's rhythm plays, and all is clear.

Jubilant Jests in the Green Glow

The squirrel wore a tiny hat,
And danced upon a fence post fat.
The robins giggled in a tree,
As leaves swirled round in glee.

A bunny hopped with great delight,
Stole the sun from day to night.
A squirrel tossed an acorn high,
It landed with a funny sigh.

The frogs played tag upon a stone,
While crickets chirped a silly tone.
The brook laughed loud with every wave,
A joyful tune that nature gave.

Amidst the grass, a worm did groove,
In earth's embrace, it found its move.
With every peep and every chirp,
A symphony of playful burp.

The Nature of Happiness Among the Pines

Beneath the pines, a secret found,
Where giggles echo all around.
A moose in shades, with style unmatched,
Waltzed in humor, quite attached.

A raccoon juggles shiny things,
While all the laughter sweetly sings.
The ants parade in tiny shoes,
Wiggling as they shake the blues.

A butterfly with polka dots,
Swirl around in silly knots.
The sunbeams tickle every leaf,
Spreading joy, erasing grief.

In frolic fields where wild things play,
Nature holds a festive sway.
With every breeze, a chuckle flows,
In merry antics, laughter grows.

Silliness in the Shade

In the shade, a turtle raced,
With a floppy hat, so out of place.
The bunnies giggled at the sight,
As he tripped and took flight.

A parrot wore a pirate's eye,
Told tall tales and made them fly.
While bees did buzz a dizzy tune,
With dance moves that made flowers swoon.

A chipmunk served a tea of grass,
To woodland friends who came to pass.
They plotted pranks on passing squirrels,
With hidden nuts in playful swirls.

With sunlit smiles and tails a-wag,
Each moment felt like a fun new brag.
In every rustling, soft embrace,
We found our joy, our happy place.

Heartwarming Larks in the Land of Leaves

In the land where leaves do sway,
Birds hold court in a bright ballet.
With feathers bright and tales so grand,
They tickle hearts across the land.

The woodpecker drummed a silly beat,
While rabbits danced on eager feet.
A hedgehog laughed and wiggled round,
Creating joy where fun is found.

A breeze blew through, a playful tease,
With whispers sweet among the trees.
Each shadow danced, a playful shade,
Inviting all for fun displayed.

In every giggle, every cheer,
The spirit of delight draws near.
As nature smiles with gleeful eyes,
We bask beneath the cheerful skies.

Glee in the Clearing

In the glade where shadows meet,
A rabbit danced on its little feet.
With twirls and hops that never tire,
He set the woods in joyous fire.

The trees did chuckle with gentle sway,
As squirrels played hide and seek all day.
A breeze burst forth with a giggling sound,
And tickled the leaves that swirled around.

Jests and Jingles in the Twilight

As dusk embraced the fading light,
A raccoon donned a mask so bright.
He juggled berries with flair and glee,
While frogs croaked tunes in harmony.

The crickets chirped their rhythmic jest,
Nature's jesters, putting laughs to the test.
With chirps and squeaks in fading glow,
They spun strange tales of the night below.

Harmony of Happiness in Nature's Embrace

Beneath the boughs where wildflowers grow,
The bees buzzed tales, sweet and slow.
With petals bright, the colors thrived,
In this merry realm, delight contrived.

The brook would giggle, tumbling clear,
Claiming secrets for all who'd hear.
While butterflies danced on the playful breeze,
Painting joy upon the trees.

Frolic Some Spirits in the Ferns

In the deep shade where ferns do sway,
Friendly spirits come out to play.
With leaps and bounds, they twirled around,
Echoing glee in every sound.

They whispered secrets of silly days,
And shared old jokes in cheerful ways.
As shadows morphed in the evening glow,
Their playful spirits decided to show.

Roars of Joy Amidst Ancient Roots

In the grove where whispers play,
Squirrels dance in their ballet.
Leaves giggle in the gentle breeze,
Nature's jest, a sweet tease.

Old oaks chuckle, their stories unfold,
While shadows frolic in hues of gold.
Sunlight tickles the forest floor,
And echoes ring, forevermore.

Forest Frolics and Fun

Beneath the boughs, a parade begins,
Frogs in tuxedos, with cheeky grins.
Bouncing deer with a twinkle in eye,
Leap over stumps, oh my, oh my!

Birds hit high notes, a comical show,
As laughter drifts where wildflowers grow.
The brook gurgles, adds to the cheer,
Nature's wit is marvelously clear.

Rhapsody in the Rustic Realm

In a kingdom of bark and leaf,
Every creature's got a belief.
Rabbits giggle, taking a leap,
While busy ants plot their next sweep.

The sun winks down, a merry friend,
Wrapping the woods in a jubilant blend.
Mushrooms nod in a playful way,
Inviting all for a hilarious day.

The Sunbeam's Laughter

A sunbeam dances on a dew-kissed morn,
While butterflies in colors are born.
A wise old turtle blinks with glee,
As playful squirrels race up a tree.

Giggles bubble up from a babbling brook,
Inviting all for a friendly nook.
The petals wink—a joyous affair,
In this woodland, so light and fair.

Revelations in Radiant Rays

Beneath the branches, whispers bloom,
Squirrels dance with much to consume.
Leaves giggle in breezy delight,
As sunbeams prance, all feels just right.

Frogs wear crowns of leafy cheer,
Jokes that travel—far and near.
Each creature joins this playful jest,
Nature's laughter, truly the best.

In shadows deep, shadows wear grins,
Mice trading puns as daylight begins.
A rabbit hops, with witty reprise,
As butterflies tease in grand disguise.

The sky chuckles, clouds puff and sigh,
Tickled by stories that drift on high.
With every rustle, a punchline shared,
In this realm of joy, how none feels scared.

Merry Meetings in the Wild

A raccoon winks with a mischievous eye,
Telling tall tales while the fireflies fly.
Bears crack jokes, oh what a sight,
While owls hoot softly, lost in the night.

Amidst the ferns, friends gather round,
Echoing giggles woven into sound.
Chirping crickets, the band of the eve,
With melodies bright, it's hard to believe.

Mice whisper secrets from tree to tree,
A rehearsal for comedy, oh so free!
Frogs leap in puddles, splash up delight,
Creating a splash that twinkles the night.

The sun dips low, but spirits are high,
With chuckles and banter, we reach for the sky.
In each little corner, a jest unfolds,
Under the moonlight, the laughter beholds.

Ecstasy of the Emerald Enclave

Twisting vines weave tales in the air,
Tangled in giggles, as creatures all share.
Laughter dances on emerald lanes,
Where every critter breaks loose from its chains.

Bumbling ants march to a quirky beat,
While ladybugs tap dance on tiny feet.
Whimsical whispers float in the trees,
Tickling the leaves with playful decrees.

With each rustle, a chuckle takes flight,
As playful shadows reflect in the light.
Echoes of cheer, a party of minds,
In this lush enclave, pure joy it finds.

Butterflies giggle, prancing on air,
Spreading the magic, so vivid and rare.
All creatures unite in this joyous spree,
In the emerald embrace, life's silly and free.

Cheerful Chronicles Beneath the Timber

Under the timber, where secrets collide,
Rabbits spin tales that they cannot hide.
Nutty adventures from branches they tell,
With every hiccup, we can't help but swell!

A playful gust sends leaves on the run,
Squirrels chase shadows, oh what fun!
In the thicket, giggles float like the breeze,
As chattering birds sing with such ease.

The echoes of chuckles, a story of glee,
Dancing in circles, as wild as can be.
The drumming of paws keeps perfect time,
As faun frolics in rhythm and rhyme.

Beneath the timber, we gather to play,
In the heart of the wild, we joyously sway.
Each chirp and each rustle, a comic delight,
In nature's embrace, everything feels right.

Woodland Whimsy and Warmth

In the shade where shadows dance,
Squirrels plot their little prance,
Whimsical hats upon their heads,
Joking tales of ancient beds.

Frogs croak jokes on lily pads,
While gentle breezes tease the lads,
Twisting vines play peek-a-boo,
Painting sunshine, skies of blue.

The owls hoot in pleasant jest,
As the rabbits take a rest,
Mushrooms giggle, soft and round,
As nature's laughter sweeps the ground.

Under boughs so wide and bright,
Every leaf a burst of light,
Join the fun, don't be shy,
In this woodland lullaby!

Carefree Capers in the Canopy

Swinging high from branch to branch,
Monkeys giggle, take their chance,
With a flip and tumble here,
The forest bursts with cheer.

Birds in straws try to outsing,
Each a note plays on the swing,
A pirate parrot, bold and loud,
Makes the trees laugh, oh so proud.

Frogs in hats hop left and right,
Chasing dreams with sheer delight,
Every splash, a joyful spree,
In the roots, they sip their tea.

Sunlight filters, warm and bright,
Crafting moments pure delight,
Join the dance, hear the call,
In these woods, there's fun for all!

The Joyful Chorus of Crickets

When the sun sinks low and shy,
Crickets croon a lullaby,
In the grass, their tiny feet,
Tap a rhythm, oh so sweet.

Fireflies join the lively show,
Glowing sparks begin to glow,
Synchronized in perfect cheer,
Nature's music fills the sphere.

With a leap, a gallant thread,
A chorus sung, all fears shed,
Flickering lights and buzzing tunes,
Whispers danced beneath the moons.

And so the night spins its spell,
In their world, all laugh and dwell,
A symphony of joy and play,
In the heart of night's ballet!

Blissful Voices in Bloom

Petals rustle, soft as sighs,
As bees hum sweetly in disguise,
With cheer they flit from bloom to bloom,
Their buzzing whispers chase the gloom.

Wandering winds tell jokes so quaint,
While smiling flowers start to paint,
Colors bright, a joyous spree,
In nature's brush, pure jubilee.

Tiny ants with tipsy grace,
March to rhythms, join the race,
Over hills of fragrant bliss,
Nature's frolic wrapped in kiss.

From dawn till dusk, and dusk till dawn,
In this garden, joy is drawn,
Come and play, hear the bloom,
In the laughter that's in room!

Gleeful Gatherings in the Glorious Green

In the shade where shadows play,
Bright colors dance in soft array.
Giggles twirl like drifting leaves,
As mischief hides behind the eaves.

Squirrels chatter with silly glee,
While laughter spills from every tree.
Butterflies flutter, jokes they weave,
In a breeze that makes us all believe.

Under branches, the joy takes flight,
Tickling toes in pure delight.
Friends share tales of whims that tick,
As moments turn from slow to quick.

With every chuckle, the world grows bright,
In this gathering of hearts so light.
The green embraces our fun-filled crew,
As echoes of joy come shining through.

Euphoria Framed by Foliage

In a realm where sunlight beams,
Creative chaos reigns it seems.
With each grin, the skies break free,
Sprinkling cheer like petals from a tree.

Around the trunks, we spin with glee,
As squirrels roll their eyes at me.
Jokes bounce off the bark so clear,
And fill the air with vibrant cheer.

Shadows stretch in playful jest,
While happy hearts compose their quest.
With laughter like a warm embrace,
Each moment blossoms, wild and chaste.

Under canopies of twisting vines,
Joyful echoes form the lines.
In this lovely, leafy blend,
We find the magic never ends.

Celebration Beneath the Sunlit Sky

Beneath the branches, sunlight beams,
Unlocking all our wildest dreams.
With a skip, we join the throng,
Singing sweetly, a merry song.

The grass is soft, our feet collide,
Like tickled butterflies that glide.
A swarm of giggles fills the air,
Around us, joy is everywhere.

Friends elevate the spirits high,
As whispers blend with a cheerful sigh.
A parade of smiles dances in,
In nature's stage, our hearts begin.

With every wink and silly dance,
We cast away the mundane trance.
The sun breaks forth through greenest leaves,
In this wonderland, no one grieves.

Grinning Gatherings of Gleeful Souls

Amidst the boughs where sunlight beams,
We weave our laughter into dreams.
Ticklish toes on grassy ground,
As playful echoes shall abound.

Jesting shadows dance and play,
Where friendships bloom in bright array.
With every smile, the day unfolds,
In whispers shared, new tales are told.

Around the trees, we skip and twirl,
As nature sways in rhythmic whirl.
Each giggle spins a silken thread,
Tying our hearts like blossoms spread.

In this gathering, magic's near,
As joyous spirits persevere.
Under the green, with souls so free,
We craft a symphony of glee.

Sunny Smiles in the Shade

Beneath the leaves, we play, we cheer,
A playful breeze brings giggles near.
With shadows dancing on the ground,
Joyful echoes all around.

We chase the butterflies in flight,
Tickled by the warm sunlight.
Each grin a spark, each laugh a song,
In this moment, we all belong.

The squirrels wear tiny, cheeky grins,
As we share tales of playful wins.
A game of tag with nature's friends,
In this haven, joy never ends.

We toss our worries to the breeze,
Silly faces, we aim to please.
Sun-kissed cheeks, the joy we make,
In this shade, we laugh, we wake.

Episodes of Elation in the Earth

Rolling down the hill, oh what a sight,
With giggles bursting, hearts so light.
The flowers join in on our spree,
Waving petals, oh so free!

Ants march by in perfect rows,
Their tiny paths, where laughter flows.
We mimic their march, then take a leap,
A fit of chuckles, in our heap.

The sun dips low, the shadows play,
We tumble, giggle, dance the day.
With silly hats made of leaves,
Nature's whimsy, how it weaves!

Around us, whispers of chuckling trees,
Their branches sway, a playful tease.
We share our secrets with the ground,
In silly moments, joy is found.

Nature's Glee Adrift in Air

The clouds above start to parade,
With shapes and dreams that never fade.
A giggling breeze rushes by,
Whistle tunes and joyful sighs.

Silent breezes spark a game,
Catch them quick, we're wild and tame.
Fluffy clouds hold laughter's trace,
A fairytale within this space.

The sunbeams tickle leaves all day,
Nature's laughter in the fray.
We dance along the winding path,
Every step ignites a laugh.

The whispers play, the shadows blend,
At every turn, we find a friend.
The joy erupts, blooming bright,
In the air, pure delight.

Lighthearted Larks Under the Blue

In open fields, we gladly roam,
The world our stage, we feel at home.
With every step, we spin and twirl,
This life's a dance, let the joy unfurl.

With daisies tucked behind our ears,
We chase the sun, we banish fears.
A chorus sings of playful cheers,
Each fleeting moment, we hold dear.

The sky, a canvas painted bright,
Where laughter dances with pure light.
We share our dreams on wings of air,
In this space, we float without care.

With every heartbeat, we embrace,
This joyous world, this happy place.
Together here, we find our tune,
Under the warm and smiling moon.

Mischief and Merriment in the Meadow

In fields where daisies dance around,
A ticklish breeze whispers, 'Don't make a sound!'
Squirrels play hide and seek so fast,
While butterflies giggle, their joys amassed.

Beneath the sun, a rabbit hops,
Chasing his shadow, he never stops.
Grass stains on trousers, giggles in air,
Joy spreads like sunlight, everywhere!

A bumblebee buzzes with silly cheer,
Dancing through flowers, but never near.
With each tiny stumble, he rolls with glee,
In the meadow's play, wild and free!

Laughter ricochets off the trees nearby,
As friends make up stories, oh my, oh my!
The day slips away without a care,
In mischief and merriment, joy is rare!

Childlike Wonder Among the Willows

Beneath the swaying branches, shadows leap,
Where secrets of children are never asleep.
A muddy pair of shoes, adventure calls,
In giggles and whispers, delight never stalls.

Frog jumps in puddles, making a splash,
With friendly little giggles and a joyful dash.
Paper boats sail on the shimmering pond,
With dreams like the ripples, and laughter so fond.

Clouds drift above like cotton candy,
As young hearts play games, their spirits so dandy.
A breeze carries chuckles from girl and boy,
In the heart of the willows, they discover pure joy!

The world spins in colors, vibrant and bright,
Each moment a treasure, each laugh a delight.
Among the tall trees, with whispers of fun,
In childlike wonder, they bask in the sun.

Enchanted Giggles on the Trail

Down the winding path where wildflowers bloom,
Two friends in their sneakers escape everyday gloom.
They trip over roots, then stumble a bit,
Each fall is a giggle, each bump is a hit.

A parrot above squawks a raucous tune,
While chipmunks join in, a playful commune.
Snickers and snorts from a nearby stream,
As laughter dances in sunlight's warm beam.

The trail leads to wonders, secrets untold,
With every twist and turn, new stories unfold.
A stick becomes a wand, a crown from a leaf,
Imagination takes flight, beyond all belief!

With echoes of joy in the forest's embrace,
Adventures abound at a merry pace.
As twilight descends, their spirits take flight,
In enchanted giggles, their hearts feel so light.

Amusement Among the Aged Oaks

In the shade of giants, shadows play,
Where laughter ripples like the end of day.
An owl hoots softly, with wisdom and fun,
As friends swap stories, each sillier than one.

The acorns drop, bouncing on heads,
Creating a ruckus where silliness spreads.
A game of charades, with trees as their stage,
This woodland performance, an age-old sage.

Whimsical whispers dance on the breeze,
Carried by squirrels, performing with ease.
With every rustle, a giggle they share,
Amongst the aged oaks, there's laughter in the air.

The sun dips below, painting skies with a sigh,
As shadows grow long, and enchantments fly high.
In this joyous retreat, where memories blend,
The amusement continues, never to end.

Sunshine's Grin in a Forest of Dreams

Under golden beams they play,
Squirrels dance, chasing the day.
Whispers of joy, in the breeze,
Tickles of light among the trees.

A rabbit hops, with a giggle sound,
In this green world, smiles abound.
The leaves above, they rustle and sway,
As shadows jiggle in a playful way.

Beneath the boughs, secrets unfold,
Each twist and turn, a tale retold.
Dandelions burst, like confetti bright,
A festival of fun in warm sunlight.

With every step, a chuckle erupts,
Nature's humor, it sweetly disrupts.
In this embrace, joy springs alive,
Where dreams take flight and spirits thrive.

The Joyful Flock Beneath the Sky

Feathers fluffed in vibrant hues,
Chirping jokes, it's all good news.
The sun above, a spotlight shines,
As birds perform in funny lines.

With each flutter, laughter flows,
As little wings tickle their toes.
The clouds play tag, so soft and white,
Creating a stage for pure delight.

A pecking party in the grass,
Where tiny feet just love to pass.
Every chirp is a punchline bold,
In this bright theater, pure joy unfolds.

The breeze carries a playful tune,
With giggles rising, morning to noon.
And as the flock takes to the air,
Their giggles echo, floating with flair.

Meadow Melodies of Merriment

Flowers sway to a joyful beat,
Bees buzzing by, what a treat!
Butterflies twirl, in a colorful spin,
In this meadow, where fun begins.

A silly ant in a tiny hat,
Marching proudly, imagine that!
The grasses chatter, secrets to share,
As hoots and croaks fill the air.

With a bounce and a leap, frogs collide,
In puddles of laughter, side by side.
Dancing shadows at dusk light the scene,
Change of colors, a vivid routine.

In this place of whimsy and cheer,
Every moment, we hold so dear.
The melody rings, a sweet refrain,
In a patch of joy, we dance in the rain.

Snickers among the Sycamores

Beneath the trees, giggles abound,
Whispers of humor, all around.
Branches sway, with a teasing flair,
As squirrels prance without a care.

A raccoon peeks, with a cheeky grin,
In a game of hide and seek, he'll win.
The shadows play tricks, tickling toes,
While sunshine sprinkles, all that it sows.

With each rustle, a ticklish breeze,
Mischievous moments frame the trees.
Nature's jesters, in feathery coats,
Send ripples of laughter, causing giggles afloat.

As night falls, the stories take flight,
Bringing joy in the soft twilight.
In the stillness, chuckles remain,
Connected by whimsy, a sweet, gentle chain.

Folk Tales of Laughter Among the Daisies

In the meadow where daisies dance,
A squirrel stole a bird's bright pants.
The rabbit laughed till he turned pink,
As bees buzzed around, they'd wink.

A wise old fox shared silly tales,
Of frogs who wore boots and sails.
With every chuckle, the flowers swayed,
As sunshine painted the merry parade.

The daisies whispered secrets sweet,
Of mischief they caused with little feet.
A ladybug laughed without a care,
Spinning tales of acorns in the air.

When twilight fell, a giggle combined,
With stars above, peace intertwined.
And in that field of joyful beams,
Laughter echoed within their dreams.

Serenades of Serenity in the Sylvan Realm

In a grove where willows sway,
A raccoon sang the blues all day.
With a wink and a twirl, he'd prance,
Making shadows dance in a merry chance.

The owls hooted, sharing glee,
As chipmunks juggled acorns with glee.
Each laugh rang out through echoing trees,
Bringing joy like a sweet summer breeze.

The gentle brook chimed in tune,
As frogs croaked a rustic croon.
With every splash, the sprites would cheer,
A whimsical world, so bright and clear.

When twilight painted the sky like ink,
The forest wrapped in a hush to think.
Yet, giggles echoed through branches above,
Serenading the night with joy and love.

Whispers of Joy in the Trees

High above where branches twist,
The parakeets held a feathered fist.
With goofy flips and playful shouts,
They painted laughter, amidst their routes.

The wind would join, a gentle tease,
Tickling leaves with a soft breeze.
Squirrels swinging played peek-a-boo,
While rabbits chuckled like they often do.

Underneath the towering pines,
A turtle told the best of lines.
With walnuts cracking, a chorus sang,
As flavors of joy in the woods sprang.

When dusk embraced these joyous sounds,
Shadows danced on the hallowed grounds.
And whispers of cheer in the twilight mixed,
Creating a melody that humor fixed.

Serenade of the Swaying Leaves

Among the branches, shadows play,
A breeze tiptoes, making leaves sway.
Chasing giggles of tiny sprites,
While sunny patches bring delight.

The leaves rustle, a secret pact,
As playful winds begin to act.
A mishap here, a tumble there,
Sprinkling joy like confetti in air.

Down below, a hedgehog rolled,
In laughter's embrace, he found his gold.
With acorns raining in gentle bursts,
The forest breathed in joyful thirst.

As stars peeked through the leafy dome,
The night wrapped laughter like a warm home.
In that sanctuary, spirits twinkled bright,
With echoes of fun filling the night.

Smiles Beneath the Rustic Ceiling

In the shade where shadows play,
Giggles dance in the light of day.
Breezes tickle the gnarled trees,
Stories swirl with a teasing breeze.

Frogs croak jokes in merry sound,
Beetles boogie around and around.
The sun winks down with a cheeky glare,
While squirrels skip with a carefree air.

Colors paint the blooms so bright,
As butterflies flit in pure delight.
Amid the leaves, a rabbit grins,
Joining in where the fun begins.

Festivities Among the Flora

Buds burst forth with a laughing hue,
As nature joins in the jolly view.
Honeybees buzz with a playful cheer,
While daisies nod, they've no fear.

A fern's frond sways in a jive,
While critters frolic and come alive.
The sun shines bright, it's quite a scene,
With petals glimmering in shades of green.

Hummingbirds zip with speedy grace,
Engaging flowers in a cheeky chase.
In the midst of all, let's shout hooray,
And savor the joy of a splendid day!

Wet Leaves and Warm Hearts

Raindrops tumble from above,
While puddles giggle, oh what love!
Children splash in a gleeful ballet,
Making memories that dance and sway.

An old cat naps on a wooden seat,
Dreaming of tides and fish to meet.
With each drip, a comedic tale,
Of adventures wild in the dampened trail.

Mossy stones with a real charade,
As clouds parade in an endearing jade.
Whispers of warmth through the wet terrain,
Bring smiles that spark like drops of rain.

Whimsical Whispers of the Wind

The breeze tells secrets to blooming flowers,
As dandelions dance in sunlit hours.
Leaves sway with laughter that's light and free,
A frolic of whispers that carries a glee.

Twirls of petals as they twine and spin,
Nature's jesters, they draw us in.
Clouds play peekaboo high in the sky,
Riding on giggles that soar and fly.

Nature chuckles in a playful tune,
While shadows waltz beneath the moon.
With each gust, a mischievous call,
A whimsical journey, enchanting us all.

Serene Smiles on Sunlit Trails

Beneath the curves of leafy shade,
Giggling echoes cascade and fade.
With each soft whisper of the trees,
Jokes bounce lightly on the breeze.

Squirrels scamper, tails a-flick,
Playing tag, they're oh so quick.
A woeful turtle joins the fun,
Rolling laughs 'til day is done.

Sunbeams dance on puddles round,
Mirth awakens in the sound.
Nature chuckles, skies so blue,
A comedy show just for you.

So join the jest beneath the sun,
With every trail, joy's never done.
In this green world, let spirits soar,
Serene smiles lead to laughter's door.

The Gleeful Gatherers of Greenery

In fields where daisies bloom so bright,
A troop of friends takes flight,
Chasing butterflies with glee,
As happiness flutters wild and free.

They toss around a leafy crown,
Joking, twirling, never down.
With every step, a wink, a grin,
The merriment is sure to win.

Dandelion seeds start to float,
Laughter trails like a happy note.
Riddles spun beneath a bough,
Cheerful hearts, oh, take a bow!

Gather round, the forest sings,
Joyful sounds that nature brings.
In every rustle, smile, and cheer,
The gleeful gatherers know no fear.

Radiant Roots of Revelry

Underneath the willow's sway,
Laughter blooms at close of day.
Tickled leaves and shy sunbeams,
Whisper secrets, silly dreams.

Ants march on a merry quest,
Building castles, doing their best.
While rabbits plot a playful prank,
With hops and flips, they fill the bank.

Flowers chuckle, petals sway,
Join the dance of bright ballet.
Under roots where wild things play,
Radiant joy is here to stay.

So join the riot, sing with glee,
Nature's spirits wild and free.
In this realm where fun takes flight,
Revelry blooms both day and night.

Exuberance Encircled by Nature

In a circle of friends, we stand,
Giggles echo, hand in hand.
With the breeze, we share our glee,
Nature smiles, just wait and see.

Bouncing berries, ripe and sweet,
Make our laughs a joyful treat.
Chasing shadows, racing skies,
With each twist, a new surprise.

Sunshine paints the morning bright,
Voices ring from left to right.
Frogs croak jokes by the pond,
Joyful hearts, of this we're fond.

So gather here, the wild and free,
In every laugh, it's plain to see.
Exuberance in every tree,
Nature's joy is our decree.

Joy Beneath the Trees

Squirrels chase with nuts in tow,
A dance of mischief, oh what a show!
Breezes giggle, leaves all sway,
Nature's jesters, brightening the day.

Beneath the boughs, shadows play,
Frogs croak tunes in a funny way.
A chorus of chirps, a playful breeze,
Creating laughter among the leaves.

Children run, their joy so sweet,
Finding wonders at their tiny feet.
A game of tag with shadows cast,
Moments like these, forever last.

Oh, the tales the trees could share,
Of giggles echoed, light as air.
In the heart of woodlands, spirits blossom,
This merry symphony, forever awesome.

Whispers of Cheer Among the Leaves

In the dappled light, secrets swirl,
Tiny wonders invoke a twirl.
Gentle whispers, joy takes flight,
Chasing shadows, delightfully bright.

A chubby bird attempts to sing,
Wobbling slightly on a spring.
The grasshoppers join in with glee,
A frolicsome band beneath each tree.

Faces gleam with sunny streaks,
Imitating nature's funny peaks.
Beneath the green where giggles bloom,
The woods embrace with joyful room.

Rustling leaves share tales of cheer,
Each twist and turn brings laughter near.
In the forest, smiles vie with the sun,
A playful world where we're all one.

Giggles in the Glade

In the glade where wildflowers peek,
The bumblebee buzzes a happy sneak.
Mushrooms giggle in their tiny homes,
Swaying gently as the sunlight roams.

A frolic of foxes, tails up high,
Playing tricks as they zip by.
The rustling brush, a playful cheer,
Nature's antics, loud and clear.

Little feet plant with glee,
Chasing butterflies, oh so free.
The sun-drenched air fills with smiles,
Joy echoes across the miles.

In the heart of green, we find delights,
Adventure beckons in playful flights.
Beneath the sun and shade so wide,
Giggles in the glade are our joyful guide.

Chuckles in the Shade

Under branches, secrets hide,
Where bothers fade, and fun's our guide.
The breeze composes playful tunes,
Dancing lightly with happy boons.

A rabbit trips on its own two feet,
Making faces no one could beat.
As frogs play leap, to a silly song,
Echoing giggles where they belong.

Bright butterflies flutter with flair,
Painting joy in the warm summer air.
Every rustle spins tales anew,
As chuckles in the shade renew.

Moments shared beneath the skies,
With secret laughter and joyful sighs.
The shade embraces with open arms,
Keeping us safe from all the harms.

Riotous Revelry on the Forest Floor

Bouncing squirrels race up trees,
Dropping acorns with the breeze.
Frogs in hats jump to a tune,
While mushrooms dance beneath the moon.

Sassy foxes play hide and seek,
Each little chirp is quite unique.
A caterpillar spins a jest,
While bees buzz in their fancy vest.

Picnics spill with fruit and cheer,
As giggles bubble loud and clear.
The ground is filled with playful paws,
Celebrating with nature's applause.

Underneath the leafy spread,
Whispers of joy, where no one's led.
In this haven, all are free,
To share a smile, to share a spree.

Heartfelt Chuckles Under the Arch

A raccoon dons a tiny hat,
With joyous friends, they squawk and chat.
Nearby, a parrot sings a song,
As all the critters dance along.

Ducks wear shades, a stylish crew,
With clumsy steps, they waddle too.
Under the branches, laughter flows,
As sunlight sparkles on their toes.

The groundhog plays the jester's part,
With silly jokes that warm the heart.
While ladybugs spin in delight,
In this whimsical, joyous sight.

Trees chuckle with a rustling sound,
Echoes of fun dance all around.
With laughter shared and glee in sight,
The forest glows with pure delight.

Nature's Giggle Fest

Crickets chirp, their symphony,
As butterflies swirl joyfully.
A wild hare hops with playful pride,
While the flowers sway side to side.

Witty owls chuckle from above,
As they share tales of forest love.
The grass bends low with every pun,
As shadows merge, and day is done.

Each pebble throws a witty line,
With every twirl, nature's design.
Giggling streams rush past with glee,
Where every ripple's wild and free.

In this land where smiles collide,
All creatures join for a joyous ride.
With hearts that burst and joy so strong,
This fest of fun will not seem long.

Resonance of Rapture in the Grove

Beneath the boughs where dreams take flight,
A jester's cap is such a sight.
Rabbits skip in a merry line,
With whispers sweet as aged fine wine.

The air is thick with sweet delight,
Echoing giggles throughout the night.
Fireflies twinkle, a lively show,
While tree frogs croak their hearty pro.

Soft moss cushions every fall,
As critters gather, one and all.
With every leap and frolic found,
The spirit of joy knows no bound.

So here's to fun in whispered tones,
The heart of nature sings and moans.
From stem to stem and root to leaf,
We thrive in joy, beyond belief.

Mirth in the Meadow

In the meadow, silliness grows,
Bouncing bunnies strike funny poses.
The butterflies giggle as they fly,
While the daisies whisper and sigh.

Tickling grass beneath our feet,
Chasing giggles, oh what a treat!
Friends rolling down in pure delight,
Painting the day with colors so bright.

A squirrel dressed up in a turtleneck,
Scurrying fast, what the heck!
Each chuckle echoes through the air,
Joy mixed with sunshine everywhere.

With each crack of a silly joke,
We gather 'round, hearts wide open.
In this meadow, we find our bliss,
Sharing smiles we never could miss.

Echoes of Delight in the Grove

In the grove where tall trees sway,
Funny whispers brighten the day.
A parrot mimics with a cheeky grin,
Its playful antics make us spin.

Rabbits hopping like they're on fire,
Their silly antics never tire.
Sunlight dances on the leaves,
As laughter wraps around like sleeves.

With every tickle from the breeze,
We share our stories that tease and please.
A bear in a hat joins our fun,
Creating memories under the sun.

As echoes of giggles fill the space,
We take turns, each creating our place.
In this grove, we leave our cares,
With gleeful hearts, nothing compares.

Serenades of Smiles Under the Branches

Beneath the branches, shadows flip,
We gather 'round for a silly trip.
A cat in sunglasses takes a pose,
As we share tales that nobody knows.

The breeze hums an off-key tune,
While squirrels host a funny cartoon.
Each branch a stage for our whimsy,
Transforming moments into frenzy.

We play peekaboo with the sun,
Playing games, oh this is fun!
Frogs join in with their own croaks,
Creating laughter, like gentle jokes.

Under the branches, we sing out loud,
Embracing joy, we're all so proud.
With every giggle vines twist and sway,
In our hearts, we forever stay.

The Dance of Joyful Shadows

In the twilight, shadows sway,
Dancing creatures in a funny play.
A fox in sneakers claims the floor,
Joking, laughing, as we roar.

Chasing fireflies, laughter glows,
We twirl and spin, as the cool wind blows.
A raccoon wearing a jester's hat,
Makes us chuckle, imagine that!

The moon shines bright, a cheeky tease,
Inviting stars to dance with ease.
Our hearts are light, our spirits high,
In this playful world, no need to lie.

As shadows flicker and dances unfold,
We weave happiness, bright and bold.
Tonight we revel, forever friends,
In joy's sweet dance, the fun never ends.

Giggles Amidst the Branches

Squirrels dance in whimsical glee,
Dropping acorns, as sprightly as can be.
Birds tweet jokes from high above,
Nature's laughter, a chorus of love.

In the shade where the shadows play,
The breeze whispers secrets, come join the fray.
Children tumble, their faces aglow,
Every twist and turn, a delightful show.

Beneath the leaves, mischief brews,
A frog jumps high, it's quite the muse.
With every croak, giggles ignite,
In this playful scene, all feels right.

As clouds drift by, shapes come and go,
A bunny lopes, quite the comic show.
Joy fills the air, it's catchy and true,
In this branchy sanctuary, laughter renews.

Mirth in the Meadow

In fields where daisies sway and twirl,
A puppy runs, causing quite a whirl.
Tumbleweeds roll in playful pursuit,
Every moment is fun, absolute.

A butterfly winks, with colors so bold,
While a turtle plods, moving slow but gold.
Children hide, playing peek and squeak,
Each giggle spills, oh what a cheek!

Under a sunbeam's warm embrace,
A rabbit hops, adding to the race.
With a whoop and a clap, spirits rise,
Here joy dances, painting the skies.

Grass tickles tummies, they roll and fall,
Every echoing chuckle, a sweet call.
Mirthful moments, alive and bright,
In nature's peaceful arms, pure delight.

Chortles Beneath the Boughs

The trees wear smiles, their leaves a-shake,
As critters gather for fun's sweet sake.
A raccoon jests, with eyes all agleam,
A world of wonder, a whimsical dream.

Branches sway, like dancers in tune,
While shadows play games beneath the moon.
A gentle wind carries giggles around,
In this forested haven, joy is found.

Frogs serenade in the twilight's glow,
Their chorus of chuckles, a charming show.
Fireflies flicker, like stars up close,
Each blink a chuckle, as if to boast.

Beneath the boughs, spirits take flight,
Where the playful roam, all feels so right.
Nature's comedy, a delightful sight,
In the heart of the woods, laughter ignites.

Frolic Under the Open Sky

Beneath the wide dome, where kites take wing,
Children chase dreams, their hearts dance and sing.
A picnic spread brings smiles galore,
With sandwiches flying, oh what a score!

Running through meadows, shoes lost in the chase,
Each stumble and tumble, a light-hearted race.
Giggling echoes through bright summer air,
As butterflies twirl, carefree without care.

A puppy chases shadows, they dive and dart,
While laughter spills forth, a joyous art.
Grapevines weave tales of marvels and cheer,
In this cheerful realm, all feels near.

Clouds gather 'round, puppets in blue,
Crafting tales anew, as they drift and skew.
With each happy moment, a story unfolds,
In the treasure of time, joy never grows old.

Frothy Giggles in the Flower Bed

Bumblebees dance in a dainty swirl,
Petals tumble, as if in a twirl.
Frogs in the pond sing a silly tune,
While daisies giggle beneath the moon.

A squirrel slips with a nut in tow,
Tumbling over in a comic, slow show.
Butterflies flutter, their patterns a jest,
In this flower bed, everyone's a guest.

The daisies whisper, 'Watch out for crumbs!'
While ants march by, playing silly drums.
The garden's alive with those happy embraces,
Where every creature wears funny faces.

So come join the fun, let your worries shed,
In the frothy giggles of the flower bed.
With laughter and mirth, we dance and we play,
In this whimsical world where joy finds its way.

Beneath the Boughs of Bliss

Under the trees where shadows take flight,
Squirrels perform acrobatics, what a sight!
Branches giggle as they sway in the breeze,
While the whole forest chimes in with ease.

A wise old owl hoots, 'Goodness, what fun!'
As tiny mice chase, under the sun.
The blushing blooms toss their heads in delight,
Creating a chorus that sparkles the night.

With a rush of leaves, the jokes unfurl,
Like twinkling stars in a whimsical swirl.
Frolicking creatures share stories and glee,
In this woodland jive, so wild and free.

When laughter erupts 'neath the boughs of bliss,
Everything sparkles with an enchanting kiss.
In every nook, where the jesters convene,
A world full of wonders waits to be seen.

The Playful Spirit of the Wilderness

In the heart of the woods, where the paths are unclear,
The creatures emerge, to spread all the cheer.
Foxes are prancing with merriment bold,
While raccoons giggle, 'We're never too old!'

Dancing on streams, the minnows do splash,
As branches above sway, forming a bash.
The deer play hide and seek with great flair,
With grinning rabbits who haven't a care.

Every nook has its quirks, full of tease,
With nature's own jesters amused as you please.
Twisting vines whisper secrets of jests,
Where the playful spirit of joy never rests.

So wander these woods, let your worries go,
In the wilderness' laughter, feel the glow.
With the beat of the earth, you'll bounce and you'll soar,
In this joyful expanse, who could ask for more?

Melodies in the Canopy's Embrace

Up in the branches, the birds start to sing,
With giggles and chirps, they welcome the spring.
The sunbeams dance, creating a show,
As shadows skip lightly, in playful flow.

Greeneries rustle, as breezes collide,
While insects hum tunes, with nowhere to hide.
The canopy sways in a choral delight,
With melodies echoing deep through the night.

As sunflowers sway, knights of the field,
In their golden armor, they laughter yield.
Chasing each other through petals and vines,
In this laughter-filled place, joy brightly shines.

So join in the frolic, and let yourself soar,
Where melodies linger, and spirits explore.
In the canopy's embrace, all troubles erase,
With each joyful note, find your happy place.

Merrymaking in Nature's Embrace

In the meadow where shadows play,
Squirrels dance and frolic all day.
Flowers giggle with colors bright,
As butterflies twirl in pure delight.

Breezes whisper silly jokes,
While the brook sings tunes of croaks.
Every rustle, a playful tease,
Nature's joy carried by the breeze.

Playful Spirits in the Glade

In the glade, the shadows prance,
Wildflowers join in the dance.
Chirping birds play tag above,
Nature's playground filled with love.

A cheeky fox with a sly grin,
Pops out to play, where fun begins.
The trees sway to the laughter's tune,
As rabbits hop 'neath the silver moon.

Grins in the Greenery

Here in the green, where giggles grow,
Sunbeams tickle the earth below.
Ladybugs wear their spots like crowns,
And bumblebees buzz playful sounds.

A frog leaps high with a joyful splash,
While leaves rustle in a cheeky flash.
Every corner holds a hidden cheer,
In nature's garden, the fun is near.

The Delightful Symphony of the Wild

In the wild, where the deer frolic free,
Mirthful echoes blend with the trees.
Crickets chirp their rhythmic beats,
While owls hoot with clever feats.

The sunbeams dance, casting playful light,
As shadows gather, holding tight.
Every creature partakes in the fun,
In this symphony of life, we run.

www.ingramcontent.com/pod-product-compliance
Lightning Source LLC
Chambersburg PA
CBHW051630160426
43209CB00004B/586